LIMITLESS

24 REMARKABLE AMERICAN WOMEN of VISION, GRIT, and GUTS

by LEAH TINARI

ALADDIN
New York   London   Toronto   Sydney   New Delhi

To Mama.

Thank you for making my 1980s childhood so colorful. You will always be a vision on the dance floor, doing the mashed potato and the twist. Thank you for letting me witness the love and strength it takes to be a daughter caring for her elderly mother in the last years. You and grandma taught me so much. I am forever grateful. And THANK YOU for showing me that girls can do what boys can do in the kitchen, on the ball field, in the art gallery . . . WHEREVER!

For the last twenty years I have been making art about my life:

creating celebratory paintings serving as a visual diary, documenting my world and the people and "stuff" in it. I always felt I was the sole director and producer of my work—until one day I wasn't. I called this "motherhood."

Motherhood shifted my focus from a thirtysomething's nonstop New York City nightlife to the hilarity and struggles of bringing up a child in the city. I had this new director in my life, and I wasn't entirely sure how I felt about it. But I decided I would give it a whirl and agreed to take his cues.

As he grew, my son, Mars, became interested in a lot of subjects, as kids do, but specifically our US presidents. He had many questions; some I could answer, and with others I had absolutely no idea, which led me down the rabbit hole of presidential research.

When Mars asked me to find a poster or image of the presidents for his bedroom wall, we searched and came up empty-handed. We thought everything we found was dreary and outdated.

Cue motherhood: If I was feeling really ambitious, I would just paint all the presidents myself. Right? And so it began. But as I completed one portrait after another after another, my resentment began to grow. I had just spent months painting and researching men and only men: forty-four male portraits. I was frustrated.

Frustrated . . . but soon galvanized.

After wrapping up my presidents project, I woke one morning to the news that the actress Carrie Fisher had passed away. I was so upset, I decided to celebrate and honor her by painting her portrait.

The first time I laid eyes on Princess Leia was in *The Empire Strikes Back*. (My dad took our family and my brother's friends to see the movie for my brother David's eighth birthday. I was four.) As I painted, I wondered why the Princess Leia character had such an effect on me. And then I remembered as a little girl I really wanted to be a "Christine" or a "Samantha." I was *very* self-conscious about my name, Leah, that it wasn't more well-known or popular. It really bugged me that I could never find anything with "Leah" on it: a bike license plate, a key chain, a toothbrush, a wristband, *anything*. (You know, the stuff that's important.)

When I saw Princess Leia on the big screen with her unusual hairstyle and cool outfit, I was mesmerized. She was my kind of princess: not cheering from the sidelines waiting to be rescued, she was "in it," a fighter in the rebellion against evil and for her people's freedom. Leia was adored, fierce, phenomenal—and immediately all of those feelings about my name melted away. I wanted to *be* her. I felt proud to share her name, proud to have *my* name, and proud to be a girl. Yes, it was spelled differently, but from that day forward when people asked me if I was named after Princess Leia, you bet I was.

Princess Leia helped me hold my head up high with confidence. I left the theater feeling reassured that it was okay to be a tomboy, to play baseball with the boys, to wear my brother's hand-me-down jeans and Yankees jacket, and to be part of the action.

Yes, Carrie was playing the character Princess Leia on the big screen, but as I researched her for this project, my forty-year-old self found I admired the person Carrie for the same reason my four-year-old self was so enamored of her as Leia.

Carrie Fisher was a fearless fighter and advocate, both on the screen and off. To me Carrie and Leia are one, and I am grateful to them for inspiring my path through girlhood.

The very moment I completed her painting, I knew I had a new project brewing. I was inspired by this portrait of a complicated woman, and I needed to paint another and another and another. I wanted to curate a group of American women, some more well-known than others, but all equally dynamic doers, makers, creators, innovators, and fighters for love, for justice, for self.

The "American" part was a direct response to my paintings of US presidents. There is literally a "limitless" pool of remarkable women all over this world; I'm humbled by them daily. However, I decided to keep my choices homegrown, and I began researching American women: from Ray Eames (yes, Ray, not Charles), the *equal* contributor and designer behind the Eames empire and design legacy, to Yuri Kochiyama, a Japanese American who, while forced into an internment camp with her family, inspired other girls in her camp to write letters to the Japanese American GIs fighting for the United States of America, the very country that had interned her and her family.

I wanted to celebrate each of these women's vision, uniqueness, and perseverance, to learn more about them and share their achievements with a larger audience. Perhaps most important, I wanted my son, Mars, and other boys to know that these women could be role models or heroes for them. It should be inconsequential that they are female. What does it matter? They are people, they are humans doing meaningful things, and they deserve to be honored, respected, and remembered.

The title of this book rings so true to me. These women's capabilities are endless, their possibilities of greatness have no measure, and the number of remarkable women grows every day, with every new girl striving and paving her own way as an American woman. . . . They truly are limitless!

Leah Tinari

"I feel safe in the midst of my enemies, for the truth is all-powerful and will prevail."

Sojourner Truth
AMERICAN WOMEN'S RIGHTS ACTIVIST

"You have a good many little gifts and virtues, but there is no need of parading them, for conceit spoils the finest genius."

Louisa May Alcott
AMERICAN WRITER

"Lozen is as my right hand. Strong as a man, braver than most, and cunning in strategy, Lozen is a shield to her people."

Chief Victorio
LOZEN'S BROTHER

Lozen
AMERICAN WARRIOR

1840s to 1889 WARRIOR

PROPHET OF THE CHIHENNE CHIRICAHUA APACHE.

SHE inspired WOMEN and children across the very danger-ous TO GRANDE way from American forces when she crossed back to fight beside her fellow WARRIORS

LOZEN

"STRONG as a MAN, BRAVER than most, and cunning in strategy, LOZEN is a SHIELD to her people."

"Any woman who does not thoroughly enjoy tramping across the country on a clear frosty morning with a good gun and a pair of dogs does not know how to enjoy life."

Annie Oakley
AMERICAN SHARPSHOOTER

1860 to 1926 · PERFORMED FOR KINGS and QUEENS in BUFFALO BILL'S

HER 1st SHOT at 8 YRS old

[S]OLD he meat [fr]om [H]UNTING [to] pay off [h]er mom's [m]ortgage [a]fter her [D]AD DIED.

[M]ADE HER [O]WN [C]OSTUMES

· WILD WEST show. [sh]e wore SKIRTS to maintain her LADYHOOD

ANNIE OAKLEY

(WATANYA CICILLA = A LITTLE SURE SHOT)

"I said to myself, 'I have things in my head that are not like what anyone has taught me—shapes and ideas so near to me—so natural to my way of being and thinking that it hasn't occurred to me to put them down.' I decided to start anew—to strip away what I had been taught."

Georgia O'Keeffe
AMERICAN ARTIST

1887 to 1986 · ARTIST

SHE AND
ALFRED
TIEGLITZ
were
partners
in LIFE
and ART.

...PAINTER of
NEW MEXICO
landscape
NEW YORK
skyscrapers

HER...
favorite
STUDIO
was the
seat of
HER

one
of the
MOST
photographed
WOMEN of
the 20th century

A MUSE

MOTHER OF
AMERICAN
MODERNISM

FORD
MODEL-A.

"THE MEN
liked to
put me down
as the best woman
painter. I think
I'm one of the
BEST painters."

GEORGIA O'KEEFFE

"One way to open your eyes . . . is to ask yourself, 'What if I had never seen this before? What if I knew I would never see it again?'"

Rachel Carson
AMERICAN MARINE BIOLOGIST

1907 to 964

MARINE BIO-LOGIST, scientist, ecologist AUTHOR wrote

(ED). A RASS-OOTS ove-ent D) he read TIO F ON HE EPA er findings ed to NEW AWS AND AN of DDT

SILENT SPRING after WWII shifted her focus from the ocean to writing about MISUSE of PESTICIDES." 1963 testified about dangers of pesticides, inspiring to launch investigation

JFK

RACHEL CARSON

(OVED) to read Beatrix Potter and Herman Melville)

"Drama is very important in life: You have to come on with a bang. You never want to go out with a whimper. Everything can have drama if it's done right. Even a pancake."

Julia Child
AMERICAN CHEF

"Anything I can do,
she can do better."

"She is equally responsible
with me for everything that
goes on here."

Charles Eames
HUSBAND AND COLLABORATOR

Ray Eames
AMERICAN ARTIST AND DESIGNER

1912 to 1988 ARTIST, DESIGNER

FILMMAKER   ABSTRACT
                 PAINTER,
SHE   founder
MET   OF
CHARLES   AMERICAN

                 ABSTRACT
                 ARTISTS
                 group in
                 1936.

COLLAB-
ORATED   1 of the
as a   MOST
HUSBAND   famous
and   design team
WIFE   in HISTORY,
TEAM   but for many
                          of their early
experimented   PROJECTS..
with molded   CHARLES was
PLYWOOD.   credited as
Plyformed   a SOLO
Wood CO."   designer!
designed   EAMES
plints,   LOUNGE CHAIR?
stretchers
for the   RAY EAMES!
US NAVY!

"So transform yourself first . . . because you are young and have dreams and want to do something meaningful; that, in itself, makes you our future and our hope. Keep expanding your horizon, decolonize your mind, and cross borders."

Yuri Kochiyama
AMERICAN ACTIVIST

1921 to 2014

PEACE ACTIV-IST

WWII Internee
ORGANIZED
GIRLS in her
internment
CAMP
to
write
LETTERS
to the
JAPANESE
GIS
fighting the war.

fought through
the CIVIL
Liberties Act for
Gov. apology to
Japanese American
internees, it was signed
into law in 1988.

MOVED TO Harlem to a HOUSING PROJECT it inspired her to join the CIVIL RIGHTS movement! ADVOCATING for LATINO, BLACK NATIVE and ASIAN AMERICAN communities.

FRIEND OF MALCOLM X

YURI KOCHIYAMA

MOTHER of SIX!!

"OUR'S WORK IS YOURS TO BUILD..." ➔

"You don't make progress by standing on the sidelines, whimpering and complaining. You make progress by implementing ideas."

Shirley Chisholm
AMERICAN POLITICIAN

"There was no way that I could explain to dogs, friends, or parents my compelling need to return to Africa to launch a long-term study of the gorillas. Some may call it destiny and others may call it dismaying."

Dian Fossey
AMERICAN ANTHROPOLOGIST

"Bass player Carol Kaye . . . could do anything and leave men in the dust."

Quincy Jones
MULTIMEDIA IMPRESARIO

Carol Kaye
AMERICAN MUSICIAN

"I survived because they didn't realize they were dealing with a street kid. I grew up in New York, living in a four-story tenement house with community bathrooms."

Shirley Muldowney
AMERICAN AUTO RACER

1ST LADY OF DRAG RACING.

AND
1st LADY

"SCHOOL had no APPEAL to ME. ALL I wanted WAS to race UP and down the streets in A HOT ROD."

by
NHRA

iography
HEART
ike
A
WHEEL

vroom

SHIRLEY "CHA CHA" MULDOWNEY

nickname
CHA CHA

"If a song's about something I've experienced or that could've happened to me, it's good. But if it's alien to me, I couldn't lend anything to it. Because that's what soul is all about."

Aretha Franklin
AMERICAN SINGER-SONGWRITER

SINGER-SONGWRITER,
AND MUSICIAN!
of the
MOST charted female
artists

BEGAN singing
GOSPEL at her
FATHER'S CHURCH.

learned to
play the
piano
BY

OVER
112 singles
73 HOT 100
1 #1 R&B
18 Grammys
75 million
records
world-
wide!!

E
A
R

HAD
2 of
her
children
in her
MID-
TEENS

1ST FEMALE
performer to be
inducted into
THE ROCK and
ROLL HALL of
FAME

"THE
QUEEN
OF SOUL"

ARETHA FRANKLIN

"I'm usually the sparkle
in a closet full of
conservative clothes."

Betsey Johnson
AMERICAN FASHION DESIGNER

FASHION DESIGNER

SHE and ANDY WARHOL and MARY QUANT pioneers of "YOUTH-QUAKE"

EW WAVE PUNK

"girls do NOT dress for BOYS; they dress for themselves and, OF COURSE, each other!"

CARTWHEELS

oungest EVER
o get a
COTY FASHION CRITICS' AWARD

CHEERLEADER

BETSEY JOHNSON

"I've always kinda been a little outcast myself, a little oddball, doin' my thing, my own way. And it's been hard for me too, to be accepted, certainly in the early years of my life."

Dolly Parton
AMERICAN SINGER-SONGWRITER

"I would rather be funny than gorgeous, absolutely. Because it's too hard to be gorgeous, you know. I could make a stab at gorgeous as long as I had something funny to say to get out of it."

Gilda Radner
AMERICAN COMEDIAN

"Live your truth."

Tracey Norman
AMERICAN MODEL

"I believe in the theater and I believe in art. I think culture does absolutely impact our DNA. It's the one thing that gets inside of us and actually makes change."

Eve Ensler
AMERICAN PLAYWRIGHT

PLAYWRIGHT, ACTIVIST,

new yorker

survivor
OF
childhood
sexual
AND
physical
ABUSE.

FOUNDED
V-DAY
IN 1998, a
global
activist
movement
to END
violence
against
GIRLS
AND
WOMEN

raised over 100
MILLION $

PERFORMER,
AUTHOR
OF THE
VAGINA
MONOLOGUES
printed
IN
48
languages

ADOPTED
her son
at age
23, he
WAS
15.

practicing
BUDDHIST !!

EVE ENSLER

"Ultimately I think we're all looking for communal experiences—places and times that connect us to the world in meaningful and beautiful ways."

Liz Lambert
AMERICAN HOTELIER

HOTELIER FOUNDER and CREATOR OF Bunk-house GROUP

AINT CECILIA, L COSMICO, AVANA AN JOSE AN RISTON/ AJA

creates spaces that EMBRACE and CELEBRATE their local communities.

he was a lawyer n NYC DA's OFFICE nd returned ome to EXAS for a b in the ATTORNEY enerals office, ad a realization anting CHANGE! nocked THE DOOR OF FLOP-USE SAN JOSE OTEL SHE OUGHT IT WORK HARD AVEL LOT, EEP UR EYES OPEN! LOVER of MUSIC, her design encompasses

Instead OF TRYING TO REALLY DESIGN SOMETHING, IF YOU LISTEN TO THE PLACE AND MAKE SOMETHING as part of a PLACE, it becomes EASIER..." ALL of the senses

LIZ LAMBERT

"Stay afraid, but do it anyway. What's important is the action. You don't have to wait to be confident. Just do it and eventually the confidence will follow."

Carrie Fisher
AMERICAN ACTRESS, AUTHOR, AND
MENTAL HEALTH ADVOCATE

"Most comedy is based on getting a laugh at somebody else's expense. And I find that that's just a form of bullying in a major way. So I want to be an example that you can be funny and be kind, and make people laugh without hurting somebody else's feelings."

Ellen DeGeneres
AMERICAN COMEDIAN

"I'm just a human being who's moved by certain things, and if certain things break my heart, I set out to fix them."

Kimberly Peirce
AMERICAN FILM DIRECTOR

FILM DIRECTOR:

BOYS
DON'T CRY

←5 years of research!!

"ART
CHANGED
my life,
I mean,
I would
SAY
ART
saved
ME.
I
believe
that it
MADE ME
BETTER at
handling
MY LIFE"

abandoned
former
thesis after
tackling an
article
about
Brandon
TEENA, a
transgender
man who
was raped
and
murdered
he went
to Brandon's
hometown in
Nebraska to
research
the story, attending
murder trials and conduct-
ing interviews. Realization
formed "no absolute
truths" for gender
and sexual identity.

KIMBERLY PEIRCE

"We all have dreams, and if you're out there and you have a dream and you want something—you want something so bad—you've got to risk everything. You've got to risk being completely devastated if you don't achieve it, and when you fall down, you've got to get back up."

Abby Wambach
AMERICAN ATHLETE

ATHLETE · SOCCER PLAYER

FORWARD POSITION
2 time OLYMPIC
GOLD medalist
World record for
INTERNATIONAL
GOALS for both
MALE AND FEMALE !!
AT AGE 4 after
scoring 27 goals
in the 1st 3 games
she was
moved to the
BOYS' TEAM.

AMBASSADOR of
ATHLETE ALLY
nonprofit to END
HOMOPHOBIA
AND
trans-
phobia
IN SPORTS.

battled
"addiction"

"I have
never
dribbled
the whole
FIELD
and scored
a GOAL by
MYSELF."

ABBY. WAMBACH

youngest of 7 siblings, her bulldog rides a skateboard

SOJOURNER TRUTH

BORN: circa 1797 (exact date not known, as she was born into slavery), upstate New York
DIED: November 26, 1883, Battle Creek, Michigan
POWERFUL MOMENT: In 1843 she changed her name from Isabella Baumfree (her slave name) to Sojourner Truth, as she claimed, "The Spirit calls me, and I must go," and then traveled widely, preaching about the abolition of slavery.

LOUISA MAY ALCOTT

BORN: November 29, 1832, Germantown (Philadelphia), Pennsylvania
DIED: March 6, 1888, Boston, Massachusetts
POWERFUL MOMENT: Louisa volunteered to be a nurse in the Civil War, leaving her home in Massachusetts in December 1862 for Union Hotel Hospital in Washington, DC.

LOZEN

BORN: circa 1840, Ojo Caliente, New Mexico
DIED: June 17, 1889, Mount Vernon Barracks, Alabama
POWERFUL MOMENT: Stretching out her arms, palms facing the sky, Lozen started praying. When her hands tingled and her palms darkened, she could sense the direction and distance of an enemy, warning her people of danger.

ANNIE OAKLEY

BORN: August 13, 1860, Darke County, Ohio (given name: Phoebe Ann Mosey)
DIED: November 3, 1926, Greenville, Ohio
POWERFUL MOMENT: In 1875 in Cincinnati, Ohio, at age fifteen, Annie was in a shooting match against Frank Butler, a professional marksman. Butler shot twenty-four out of twenty-five birds; Annie shot all twenty-five of her birds, winning the match.

GEORGIA O'KEEFFE

BORN: November 15, 1887, Sun Prairie, Wisconsin
DIED: March 6, 1986, Santa Fe, New Mexico
POWERFUL MOMENT: Georgia's *Jimson Weed/White Flower No. 1* hung in the White House during President George W. Bush's term, and in 2014 became the most expensive painting by a female artist sold at auction, for $44.4 million.

RACHEL CARSON

BORN: May 27, 1907, Springdale, Pennsylvania
DIED: April 14, 1964, Silver Spring, Maryland
POWERFUL MOMENT: When she was ten years old, Rachel's first story about a downed fighter pilot, "A Battle in the Clouds," was published in *St. Nicholas* magazine.

JULIA CHILD

BORN: August 15, 1912, Pasadena, California
DIED: August 13, 2004, Montecito, California
POWERFUL MOMENT: During World War II, Julia was rejected by both the WAVES (Women Accepted for Volunteer Emergency Service) and the WAC (Women's Army Corps), because at six feet two inches, she was too tall. However, she was accepted to the Office of Strategic Services.

RAY EAMES

BORN: December 15, 1912, Sacramento, California
DIED: August 21, 1988, Los Angeles, California
POWERFUL MOMENT: The Eames's molded plywood chair (also known as the Low Chair Wood) was called "the chair of the century" and is still produced today.

YURI KOCHIYAMA

BORN: May 19, 1921, San Pedro, California

DIED: June 1, 2014, Berkeley, California

POWERFUL MOMENT: In 1963 Yuri met civil rights activist Malcolm X. She was with him when he was assassinated on February 21, 1965.

SHIRLEY CHISHOLM

BORN: November 30, 1924, Brooklyn, New York

DIED: January 1, 2005, Ormond Beach, Florida

POWERFUL MOMENT: In 1971 Chisholm cofounded the Congressional Black Caucus, an organization consisting of African American members of Congress who worked on issues vital to African Americans.

DIAN FOSSEY

BORN: January 16, 1932, San Francisco, California

DIED: December 26, 1985, Volcanoes National Park, Rwanda

POWERFUL MOMENT: In 1963, inspired by zoologist George B. Schaller's book *The Year of the Gorilla*, Dian took out a loan and used her life savings to take a seven-week trip to Africa, including visits to Kenya, Tanzania, and Zimbabwe.

CAROL KAYE

BORN: March 24, 1935, Everett, Washington

POWERFUL MOMENT: Carol became a professional musician in 1949 at age fifteen, and has personally taught guitar to thousands of students since then. In addition to offering tutorials and seminars, she was the educator for electric bass at UCLA's Henry Mancini Institute.

SHIRLEY MULDOWNEY

BORN: June 19, 1940, Burlington, Vermont

POWERFUL MOMENT: In 1984 Shirley was in a near-fatal crash in Montreal, shattering her legs, pelvis, and hands. After a long rehabilitation she came back in 1986, winning another National Hot Rod Association Nationals title in 1989.

ARETHA FRANKLIN

BORN: March 25, 1942, Memphis, Tennessee

POWERFUL MOMENT: Aretha was regarded as a musical child prodigy and taught herself to play piano by ear, listening to the recordings of Eddie Heywood, an accomplished jazz pianist.

BETSEY JOHNSON

BORN: August 10, 1942, Wethersfield, Connecticut

POWERFUL MOMENT: Betsey made her first garment, an apron with Scottie dogs on it, at age four. She still has it.

DOLLY PARTON

BORN: January 19, 1946, Sevier County, Tennessee

POWERFUL MOMENT: In 1995 Dolly founded the Dolly Parton Imagination Library, which gives every preschool child who signs up one book each month from the time he or she is born until the child reaches kindergarten.

GILDA RADNER

BORN: June 28, 1946, Detroit, Michigan

DIED: May 20, 1989, Los Angeles, California

POWERFUL MOMENT: In 1972 Gilda auditioned for a Toronto production of the musical *Godspell* by singing "Zip-a-Dee-Doo-Dah," a song from the Walt Disney children's movie *Song of the South*. She got the part.

TRACEY NORMAN

BORN: 1952, Newark, New Jersey

POWERFUL MOMENT: At age sixty-three Tracey became the new face of the Clairol Nice 'n Easy "Color as Real as You Are" campaign after a forty-year absence.

EVE ENSLER

BORN: May 25, 1953, New York, New York

POWERFUL MOMENT: In 2012 Eve founded the movement One Billion Rising, the largest global mass-action campaign to end violence against women and girls.

LIZ LAMBERT

BORN: September 20, 1953, Odessa, Texas

POWERFUL MOMENT: In 1995 Liz bought the run-down, ramshackle 1936 Spanish Colonial–style San José Motel and eventually renovated it and transformed it to the chic Hotel San José.

CARRIE FISHER

BORN: October 21, 1956, Beverly Hills, California

DIED: December 27, 2016, Los Angeles, California

POWERFUL MOMENT: Harvard College presented Fisher its Annual Outstanding Lifetime Achievement Award in Cultural Humanism in 2016, which honors an individual whose life and contributions to popular culture and society exemplify compassion, creativity, and honesty.

ELLEN DeGENERES

BORN: January 26, 1958, Metairie, Louisiana

POWERFUL MOMENT: Ellen was the fifteenth person, and fourth woman, to receive the Mark Twain Prize, awarded to an individual who has made a significant contribution to American humor.

KIMBERLY PEIRCE

BORN: September 8, 1967, Harrisburg, Pennsylvania

POWERFUL MOMENT: Kimberly has a BA in English and Japanese literature from the University of Chicago and credits her studies there and in the classics (especially Aristotle's *Poetics* as her inspiration) as a source of creativity.

ABBY WAMBACH

BORN: June 2, 1980, Rochester, New York

POWERFUL MOMENT: In 2015 Abby and her US women's national soccer teammates were honored with a ticker-tape parade, the first time any women's team had been celebrated in New York's famed Canyon of Heroes, for their record third World Cup title.